BURNING IN THIS
MIDNIGHT DREAM

 **bitlit**

A **free** eBook edition is available
with the purchase of this print book.

BURNING IN THIS MIDNIGHT DREAM

Louise Bernice Halfe

Coteau Books

Edited by Tim Lilburn
Cover and text designed by Tania Craan
Typeset by Susan Buck
Printed and bound in Canada

Library and Archives Canada Cataloguing in Publication

Halfe, Louise Bernice, 1953-, author
    Burning in this midnight dream / Louise Bernice Halfe.
Poems.
Issued in print and electronic formats.
ISBN 978-1-55050-665-5 (paperback).--ISBN 978-1-55050-666-2 (pdf).--
ISBN 978-1-55050-673-0 (html).--ISBN 978-1-55050-674-7 (html)

    1. Native Peoples--Canada--Residential schools--Poetry. I. Title.

PS8565.A4335B87 2016   C811'.54   C2015-907243-3
                                           C2015-907244-1

2517 Victoria Avenue
Regina, Saskatchewan
Canada S4P 0T2
www.coteaubooks.com

Available in Canada from:
Publishers Group Canada
2440 Viking Way
Richmond, British Columbia
Canada V6V 1N2

10 9 8 7 6 5

Coteau Books gratefully acknowledges the financial support of its publishing program by: the Saskatchewan Arts Board, The Canada Council for the Arts, the Government of Saskatchewan through Creative Saskatchewan, the City of Regina. We further acknowledge the [financial] support of the Government of Canada. Nous reconnaissons l'appui [financier] du gouvernement du Canada.

*This book is dedicated to my children,
Usne Josiah Butt and Omeasoo Wahpasiw
as well as my grandsons
Josiah Kesic Butt and Alistair Aski Butt.*

Josiah Kesic is holding the book, Alistair Aski is looking on.

Mom and Dad's wedding, November 4, 1939

Table of Contents

Preamble

The Truth and Reconciliation process opened the door to sharing that dark history. Truth is hard to find however. Hard to share, hard to hear. At times those stories are understandably sanitized: for the teller, for the audience, safe for polite company or church basements. These stories attempt to go deeper, but never fully plumb the depths. They are intended to share yet more of that truth. Think of all the children, and weep. Children fed to pedophile priests and nuns. Children whipped and starved. Families and communities destroyed. Generation upon generation, courtesy of the Canadian Government. Courtesy of the Canadian public.

Now we seek to define reconciliation. We must first know the deeper truth however. Celebrate the survivors and the lost. Understand the way forward. At the very least get out of the way. We will survive as a people. Rise up and be proud. Reoccupy our land. And live.

Foreword by Paulette Regan

When I was asked to write the foreword to Cree poet Louise B. Halfe-Sky Dancer's fourth book of poetry, I accepted with some trepidation. How could I do justice to these poems that invoke such a powerful mix of feelings: anger, shame, despair, confusion, love, joy and hope? With a deep sense of humility, I am honoured to write these few words. As author of *Unsettling the Settler Within: Indian Residential Schools, Truth Telling, and Reconciliation in Canada*, and through my work with the Truth and Reconciliation Commission of Canada, I have reflected deeply on the incredibly rich and generous gift that Canadians have been given by those who survived the Indian residential school system. They have shared their life memories with each other and with all of us so that together we will learn, understand, and remember. They do so in the hope that we will take action to change things so that their children, grandchildren and great-grandchildren will have better lives. This is the hard work and promise of reconciliation; it involves decolonizing ourselves, our families, our communities, our workplaces, and our country. It is everyone's work.

Reconciliation has many pathways; writing poetry is one. Louise's poems are teachings. She writes hard truths about what she and her parents suffered at the hands of the nuns and priests at residential school. She writes about secrets that haunt and silences kept, and about finding the strength to persevere. Sky Dancer's poems are teachings. She writes about her *nōhkom* and *nimosōm*, her Cree grandparents, who knew the old ways - the medicines, the pipe, the sweat lodge – and enjoyed the wealth and dignity that came from living and working on their own land. Louise-Sky Dancer's writing is both a courageous act of resistance and a reclaiming of culture, language, and the blood memory of her ancestors that despite the ravages of colonialism, is still written on her heart.

Her poems remind us that sometimes childhood memories comfort us as we recall our home, our family, our culture. These teach us about who we are and where we belong. We remember the places, sights, sounds and smells of our childhood. We treasure those special times we shared with grandparents or parents as they lovingly taught us how to walk in the world. For many residential school survivors, there are other memories too; of adults who abused them and spewed racial hatred that made them feel ashamed, confused, lonely and unloved. Memories of loss, disconnection and an unrelenting longing for the ties of family and community that have been damaged and may never be repaired. Memories of unsafe homes where the lessons of violence learned by great-grandparents, grandparents and parents in the residential schools were then inflicted on new generations of children. Survivors' life stories hold all of these memories.

These poems are testimonies of truth, justice and healing. These poems are gifts. I invite you, the reader, to read and reflect upon them with open minds and humble hearts. Then share them with others. They unsettle us in a good way. They inspire us. They give us hope.

Pete Waskewitch, Kakakon (Wilfred Chocan's grandmother) and Charlie Waskewitch. Pete and Charlie are brothers.

Dedication to the Seventh Generation

ahāw,
ōta ka-wīhtamātin ācimisowin
I will share these stories
but I will not share
those from which I will never crawl.
It is best that way.
I forget to laugh sometimes,
though in these forty years
my life has been filled
with towering mornings,
northern lights.

Sit by the *kotawān* – the fire place.
Drink muskeg and mint tea.
Hold your soul
but do not weep.
Not for me, not for you.
Weep for those who haven't yet sung.
Weep for those who will never sing.

I cannot say for sure what happened
to my mother and father.

The story said,
she went to St. Anthony's Residential School
and he went to Blue Quills.
They slept on straw mattresses and
attended classes for half a day.
Mother worked as a seamstress,
a kitchen helper, a dining room servant,
or labored in the laundry room.
Father carried feed for the pigs,
cut hay for the cattle and
toiled in the massive garden.

That little story is bigger than I can tell.

Before them were *nōhkom* and *nimosōm*.
She was a medicine woman
whose sweat lodge was hidden away,
wore prayer beads
and always had a pipe dangling
from her mouth.
nimosōm had his own car
back in the fifties
and he plowed his own land.
He was a wealthy man because
they lived in a house while we had a cabin.
He lifted the sweat rocks
for *nōhkom*.
That is as far back
as I can take you.

All the Old Man said is that
I have nothing to weep about,
compared to them.

I know now where the confusion began.
She was a tough mistress, that confusion.
We were all caught in her web.
Her history is covered in blisters, welts
and open sores. You already know that part.
We came later.
We were the children
that mother and father tried
yes, tried to raise.

How scared *nimosōm* and *nōhkom* were.
They knew what the priests, and nuns,
supervisors did at those schools.
We all left, all of us.
Confusion was in our wind.
We no longer knew
where to turn.

That is where my footsteps began
where my footprints
appear in snow, in grass.

I don't like walking backwards.

Old ones haunt my thoughts
tiny spirits that brush
the colour off my wings.
I need them now
to help others understand what happened.

It wasn't their fault.
It wasn't our fault.

Confusion was the ultimate glutton.
He came from far away
wore black robes and carried a crucifix.
He was armed with laws, blankets
and guns.
He fixed us with a treaty
that he soon forgot.

Sometimes the end is told before the beginning.
One must walk backwards on footprints
that walked forward
for the story to be told.

I will try this backward walk.

masaskon - stripped

I found myself released from residential school yet
the four walls slithered everywhere I went.
I had no regimented call
to wake up,
line up for breakfast, for dinner, for supper, for school,
and no one checking the work I did.
There were no boarding school dresses,
no tams to fight over.
I didn't know how to behave
didn't know what was expected
at the Indian Affairs homes.
I was expected to carry on
my reading, writing and arithmetic.
I didn't know how to register for class,
how to study,
how to ask.
Silence and humiliation wove my umbilical cord
in this new womb.

I wandered,
calling inside
my own name.

nimihtātēn – I grieve

I stretch the boundaries of my skin
and crucify the edges
so I have something to cling to.
A hunchback inhabits my body.
Sixty winters grips my wrists.
I've carried the turtle's shell;
it protected me far too long.
I peel it off and take a toddler's step
on this red road.

Now others ask me to turn my
skin inside out.
They want to know
how I survived this hot-coal trail.
I prefer to keep silence as my guest.
I want to keep my dead
from spilling. I don't want to deal
with their writhing wounds.
I walk behind them
trying to read their trailing guts.

āhkamēyihtamowin – perseverance

Sometimes when I walk my left ankle calls,
buckles and I stumble.
When I was young
stumbling was a frequent conversation
between my ankle and my heart.

One day my father said he'd cut the damn foot off
if I didn't walk the path like a proper child.
I knew he would.
So every day I walked
in a mindful way.

Only to lose the walk
when he told me I was like my mother
the dog in heat.
I held my chin out
and trembled
into the nightmare of my foe.

kipihtowēwin - the mouth is silenced

I am in the back alley of my thoughts.
There were no curtains, no attics,
no cellars to hide in.

My niece was two when my father
took her by her feet
and threw her across the room.
She landed on *nōhkom's* bed.
I watched this from where
no sound crept from my lips.
She was five
when she threw a pencil at his ear
after he broke a jar and slashed mother's arm.
He held a stick of fire wood over her head
while she searched for the pencil among the stack.
There were no drunken spirits
that haunted those nights
just a bowl full of angry genies.

I watched this cinema.
We huddled beneath the blanket whispering
about the great escape, as if escape to
the cabin door could be had.
The kerosene lamp and small embers
in the wood stove were all that were lit
as if the shack was a lovers den.

nanahihtamowin – to be obedient

Much like chewing *wīhkēs*, choking down Buckley's,
taking thyroid radiation
or pills for bi-polar,
injecting for diabetes or an AIDS cocktail,
I swallow this seed of blindness.

I don't consume it gladly. Rooting and digging
like a bear is not my idea
of flying with the eagle. Like my mother,
I'd rather step on the buffalo's back and
shove my memories deep into the closet.

But I promised. Promised
to stitch and sew, use colourful
embroidery thread and mend this soul.
I promised. Promised to be the company
I wanted to keep. And Promise
gripped my flesh
in her talons
when I pulled my inner eye
away from my foe.

I had heard it is so much easier
to drown or infect my liver
with wine, needles and dark alleys.
Swim into these tears
unconscious, yet awake.
Dance with these cannibals.
It is better to dance
with memory
than be noosed by the gut.

wiskas: a root that is bitter in taste

Ned Memnook

Residential School Alumni

An uncle shot his wife
left her lying behind the house
with the rifle at her side.
Their four children peered
behind the curtains.
He was never able to look at anyone.
A lake held him as he froze, standing,
clutching his traps.

One son joined the marines
a mosquito killed him in Vietnam.

In a police chase another son
hit a slough and drowned in his grave.

Their little brother slept in a flaming
house with needles, spoons, heroin and cocaine.

My cousin was left alone.

I remember them.

wāhkōhtowin – kinship

In the dark times *nimosōm*
moved like the horses he hitched to the plow.
His constant companion was Silence herself.
nōhkom stayed close, wandered to the attic
for her medicines, or crawled
into her sweat lodge.
Gone were the days when wagon loads of families
went stooking, gathering eggs, blueberry picking
and fishing.
Now they gathered to the clanking of brown bottles,
back-road trips to the bootlegger, squabbles
and fist fights along that famished road.
We, the young, were their inheritors.

wīcihitowin - helping one another

I hid in the back alley peering through the cracks
of the fence, listening to my mother calling.
My father shouting. The rain fell like bullets
and the heat bled from my eyes.
I had escaped.
Ran from the car. Left the child
my father had slammed across the room.
Our guts knew that the madness
had again descended.
I ran.

When they arrived
the pounding began.
The swearing tore our ears,
muted our tongues.
I ran.
Blind.
I ran.

I knocked on the door where the sugar-beet
bosses lived. It slammed in my face.
I walked the streets, found my way to the police,
was scolded for wandering
this slippery night.
When they arrived my father
shook his fist.

In the hotel lobby
an angel gave me a soda while I trembled
in my wetness. Other angels took me
to their bed and I slept between them.

There are times memory
allows me to sleep.

nēpēwisiwin - shame

When I was in the plundering school
I often visited the confessional.
The earth moved under me
and my knees wobbled into the pew.
A rolling plough wind darkened
the small light above the priest's head
and bile spewed from my mouth.
I'd confess. I wanted another girl's boyfriend,
lusted for his mouth
though I'd never been kissed.
Another girl and I exchanged ugly words and
she slammed the door on my bare feet.
I wanted to get even so we fought outside the gym.
I looked over Bryan's shoulder
so I could spell my words.
I vomited all over his back.
I hated the supervisor, who stole my money,
and said I was the lying thief.
I hated another one who never taught me
a girl's moon came every month and I had to hide
this visit, hide my tiny breasts. I hated the woman
who marched the little girl, who peed her bed,
in front of all of us.
My eyes swelled, leaked pus,
my morning breath foul from the confessional.
The hail marys slid down my belly.

When I returned to the log shack all that was left
was a hole filled with fireweed.
My mother, my father were strangers.
I'd watched them, how the devil took my father's hand
and lifted another woman's skirt.
My mother's feebleness fought against my uncle's
goatishness. Those spirits we consumed

brought each of us black-outs that only skid-row
dwellers would know. I make no excuse
for being a dog-in-heat or the raging beast
I'd become in this dark forest.
If I could take back that night when
I dumped my friend in the fields of nowhere
in my drunken rage
to hitchhike the thousand miles of fright, I would.
But instead, I collect these night visitors
to tell this story
to reach the heart where history placed its frost-bite
on our ragged souls.
I've dredged this artesian well and if I could
I'd burn my flesh and kill this fiend.

akāwāta - to long for

I don't want to whine about the absence of family.
For many years I walked along the eating waters
of the Elbow, the Red Deer where I eyed
their great invitation. I don't want to tell of the many miles
of gravel I yearned to run. In the forest where I snared
rabbits and nibbled bannock
is where I hid
my dreams.

Why should I complain about my back
hoeing those sugar beets
waiting to collect my pay so I could ride
the Ferris wheel in Lethbridge and not wait
beside a bar with a hungry belly and wasted wants.

What about the years and years of living
with a pack of girls
fighting over institutional dresses,
or kneeling in front of the crucifix calling
jesus to send my mother and father
to visit us from hell.
Why tell about the secrets
and their lodge
hidden in my bleached bones?

That is another winter's tale.

āhkamēyimowin - determination

I had long given up kneeling to the Christ.
I hoarded all my sins inside my turtle shell
unable to walk.
I continued to suckle.
If someone told me I was in love with myself
I'd have told them about scrubbing
the deep layers of my skin
under the eyes of
the nuns, supervisors and priests.

I thought that college social work
would become my therapist
but the computers spoke a language
ten thousand miles from Cree.
I failed so many tests,
was told I was dumber than...never mind
this mantra I already had inside my head.

My parents were unskilled laborers hard working
dedicated dirt beneath their fingernails
and I applied those gifts
scrubbing toilets waiting on tables emptying urinals
and vowed I'd get that damn degree.

On Board

I boarded with a family whose opa tried
to slip into my bed.
They were strangers happy
to take Indian Affairs orphans
and keep
my roommate and me in a cubby hole.

At school
my grades were below my belt and
extracurricular activities were scrubbing floors
at homes where I thought movie stars lived.

Or I'd be in bars
slamming back beers of joy
as real as Santa Claus.

It never occurred to me to write my family,
forgot they existed. Never received a letter,
a telephone call, but after so many years
of isolation I'd come to expect this and even
expecting this, was unexpected.

Winter Visitations

In the near distance music drifts
through the silence of the house.
The dogs wrestle and scratch the floor.
Outside weeds sway back and forth and
trees do a small circle dance.

I don't understand the sway of plants
when there is no juice in their veins
to make them bend and tremble.
You'd think they'd snap
from the breath of the winter wind.

I once pranced like a colt
and moved with the grace of a deer.
I bathed in the cool mountain falls
while my lover swam
in the nearby pool.
For those moments I was free
to absorb the frothing water.

When I looked up I saw two men
staring through the branches.
A hurricane of terror tore
through my chest.

I am often filled with ghosts
that glide through my body.
They have no business intruding
into thought or work at hand.
They hang by their feet in my lair
folding and unfolding their wings
as I hover
like a bee on a cherry blossom.

tipiskāwi-pīsim 1 - the dark moon

Like the wise women before me
I placed a mirror between my thighs ,
examined the blue clematis, the summer storm
still moist from last night's tumble. On the land
we have a crocus hill where the fall snakes hibernate.
They bask on the warmth of a large rock
before the final autumn slither
into a ground squirrel's winter hole.
My fingers move the blue flax on the grassland
between my legs,
the flower's pistil, the lovely scent of musk.
Years ago in boarding school I held a book
in front of my skirt
fumbled with a napkin
afraid my bulge would reveal the trickle
from my medicine site.

I was told never to step over men
while I was in my moon.
For a long while I thought I'd kill them, unaware
my bleeding would release a song for their starved souls.
I was told to keep my legs crossed, unaware
that I could use my scissors, engulf their slithering snakes
and receive their tiny deaths. I was never told
rivers that crossed could make a cosmic child.
It would flow,
river upon river upon river.

Age has released me from that dark moon
though she still presides in my dreams
commands my soul to learn its lessons.
I am the loosestrife growing in wet lands
a marsh marigold that blooms
in the wake of my coming.

pakosēyimo - hope

When memory wakens it becomes a flash flood
and offers no forgiveness,
I've struggled tonight with what needs to be pulled
from my gut.

It's 1971, I don't remember
the night's celebration, I wish I could speak
as if I were a white teenager and brag about that party
like so many I've heard. I had an interview that morning,
showed up with spirits
clinging to my breath and an air that said
I've been doing this all my life, joking and being familiar
with the panel of questioners. I was their troubled youth
and they wanted to save whatever grace was left.

My sister collected money,
put me on a plane for a taste of Jamaica.
I danced to mule train, witnessed song and labored
in the making of a brick school on a mountain top.
I played hard, drank that Jamaican rum,
shared my brother's motto and worked to die young.

I was the heroine of small books I read
wore a leather jacket, had the mouth
of a truck driver, but
no other speech.

māmitonēyimisow - she thinks about herself

Have you heard a buffalo snort and paw? A bear grunt?
A goose honking from the lake?
Watched a horse flick its tail and dance?
Or seen an oriole flash orange in the trees?
Felt hornet's sting?
She was all of these, that was my mother.
I knew her no other way.

I am like many, curious to know the secret lives
of parents. What did they hide in their dens?
Stained and rumpled sheets. Cast away
clothes. Lying with others.

Yet for years I hated her,
absence.
She was in the cabin but sunk into the walls.
They were prisoners of Indian Affairs.
I saw no escape. Not for them. Not for me.

Mother's life was like the rings in a tree
her skin dark, rough, bruised, exposed
but I never saw it. I pushed, demanded
that the strength that that kept her alive
would salvage both of us. In the end I gave her spoonfuls
of gentle love, kindness, respect
even though our landscape was parched.

His Name was Boy

What to say about my brother
at Blue Quills he bent to tie my skates
his fingers
stiff from the icy wind.
In the dining room he crept
up to my table and
left a sucker.
At home he drew a jack-in-the beanstalk
hopscotch and challenged me to win.

Later he had me gallop
between his legs.
Tried to sell me to our cousin
behind the plank door.

He had learned well
from the residential school
priests, and other boys.

When we were going without food and water,
lamenting in the forest
the sugar chewed both his legs
ate his kidneys and took his breath.

This March when the wind
swirled snow across the road
obscured my vision
I gave his restless spirit
tobacco.

That night in sleep, here
by my bed,
he arrived with a thump
did his little dance
and left.

Con Game

The children were meat
for the scavengers. Indian Affairs, the brick walls,
the Saints of many churches.
Filled with their disease, we ate the maggots
off their dead.
This cannibalism devoured our mother's hearth.

Yes, I followed this routine:
·clapping hands and electric light,
on our knees to give the Christ
a difficult time, no time to rub the sleep
from our eyes. Each month I counted the stars
to see how often I'd gone to mass
my heart so wanting. March to breakfast,
to the scullery, hand-peel potatoes,
wash the many pots and pans
under the supervision of the kitchen nuns.
To the laundry room to starch and iron,
to the rectory to serve the higher saints
and finally to school to swallow Europe.

In those many seasons our winds
took a turn and entered winter.
When we were released
with no hair to braid,
no language to call our own
no parent to cradle us
those storms awoke.

wīsakan - a bitter taste

iskotēwāpoy – fire water.
Indian and Northern Affairs.
The fenced residential school.
I was famished, *wīhtikow* clawed inside
the turtle I had become.
In small spaces where I cannot see
wīhtikow still lives. What my heart had eaten,
swallowed, my belly will not digest.
I am a slasher, I've cut deep
to ooze this disgrace. I've waited long
to be decapitated even though my aunt
tried to medicine me. Gave me dirt
so I could be rooted to the soil I left.
Yes, I ate her medicine.

iskotēwāpoy – literally fire water, alcohol
wīhtikow – cannibalistic spirit

sīpihkēyihta - endure

The abcess in my mouth has been present
for a long, long time. No medicine
has dulled its fire. In this journey
I've thought of you generations ahead
and your need to understand.
I wonder how a person
could enter such a fatal wound.
A hole is hard to climb out of, when there is nothing
to cling to.
There must have been a bundle that contained
moments of benevolence:
A grade two teacher who gave me
a bag of high heels that I dragged
to our log shack. The bus driver's
concern when I vomited
all over my dress. My father's frustration
with my mother's greasy cooking
that made my stomach turn.
He threw it out as I lay in bed with "romantic"
fever. He walked many miles
that night to get a ride to the hospital.
My mother overlooking the awkward stitches
on the blanket as I followed her tiny tracks.
My brother the rock, all of thirteen
driving through the pounding rain
from the Taber bars.
My pencil-throwing niece
and I huddled against him, as he drove
against the law.

kakēskimāwaso – counsel the children

I know this landslide
is hard to bear.
I've pulled the stink weeds for you
to ingest. Yet, this is one story
of many lives.
Too many lives.

maskwa - bear

Hibernating memories crawl from their den
stretch like hungry bears. I've eaten bear grease
long enough.
I've had my fill.
There are villains, scoundrels, conniving temptresses
best left to wallow in the dungeon of my heart.
I won't let them eat my soul.
They are like the grizzly that stomped
in my dream. I've provoked them
long enough.
I've sucked my marrow and banished them.
I will grow my claws,
wear the grizzly cape
and dance to my own illuminating dirt.

Picture of myself in the cowboy hat, my father holding my little sister niece
June Martha Half

kwēskī – turn around

miyoskamin, in the spring, in the forest of Kootenay Plains
the mute and her husband
invited me to their tent
showed me the dried gut, the laced fat, the dry meat
hanging from their homemade rafters.

I took my last smoke, threw the damn butt
at my uncle's door after he offered me twenty-five dollars
to feel my breasts. They were all at the same camp, the mute,
her husband, the uncle.

I wove that fat into the dry meat
and I, the child that lived far in the bush
before the sterile hallways, remembered a time
when I sliced the meat paper thin,
my father's kill, meat and fat hung with my mother's
in a wall tent.

I swallowed that flesh,
filled with this lost remembering.
My breath wild onion and my stomach doctored
by the mute's generous gift.

There were times when I hoped
I would not scorch what I salvaged.
pāhkahkos – skeleton waited for any spoils I was ready to offer.
When I lost the knowing *pāhkahkos* reached her bony hand
and made me eat this keepsake. She caressed
my carelessness, lured me into the summer hills
where she held me against her breast.
I'd attempt to look at her.

In the autumn when I was brittle
I became a slave,

a living blackout. I put out my thumb
went bar to bar
searched but
could not find the soul in any car.

It was my grandfather, *nimosōm*
who took my hand and
led me from that disobedient trail .
He gave me the gift of syllabics, the reading road,
the pipe that *nōhkom* smoked.
Head on chest
I found the healer.
The smoke lifted me in those stone hills.

tipiskāwi-pīsim 2 – night sun

The moon has been mean this month
whipping deep slashes.
I cower from her blows.
She settled on my nest of rust-covered stories
and squeezed.
I've been her erring daughter throughout
my youth. I thought I was rid of her
when I sat in the fasting lodge, watched her bleed
my useless eggs. I carried her back unaware she intended to stay.

Some visions are not worth suffering for.
I asked time and time again, please take this night.
You would think after she gifted
these shadowed years
she would release me. But I saw her still.
She was a book turning up her faces
a photo album
of child, goddess, mistress and sage.
And I her slave.

tipiyawēwisīw – ownership of one's self

I come from a breed of leaders
though I wonder if they had taken scrip
like our cousins the Métis
we would have been feathers in the wind.

In 1892, my great-grandfather, my *cāpān*
Papaschase gave this message,

My children, surrender the land.
This is a better decision for our people.
The palefaces are coming against us again,
for they are full of greed, lust and murder.
If we resist they will utterly exterminate us, yes,
even to the little ones in their mother's arms.
They are not evil.
They are like little children who are lost
because they do not understand the teachings
of the Great Spirit.
We made peace and we promised
the Great White Mother
that we would make war no more.
This is beautiful land.
It is wrong that we should stain the soil
of the land of the Red Sun with the blood
of our white brothers.
We accept this and seek a new road
for our people. We must find the pathway
that leads to the stars.
I have spoken.

Mother's father was *kihīwin*, Chief of Long Lake
her grandfather, my *cāpān*, was *pāhpāscēs*
my father's father, William

was a Saddle Lake councillor.
They were gentle men,
though I am told their will was steel.

The wind that blew from the east
saw our people herded into land rejected
by the settlers.
These grandfathers witnessed the nation's quake,
watched their children enter the brick walls.
We, the grandchildren followed.

I was called One Who Speaks With One Mouth
papēyakitōn, always searching
behind the questions.
But I never inquired enough how to find my way.
I stumbled within this silenced history.

nīcimos – boyfriend

I didn't know how to secure my mouth on another soul
didn't know how to cradle a head against my chest
and caress his hair. In the middle of the night
or before the sun arose I'd stumble out of the blankets
drag my arthritic heart through the streets
and suffocate into my pillow.
My big heavens searched their skies:
blue eyes, brown ones, green ones
some tenderness where I could drown my hollow
cry. My chin sought those hands
that would turn my world.
My body wanted more than one night
of mingy and feckless lust. So when my beloved
walked through the forest the clouds burst
and I fell into the flow of the creek that took me
to his teepee in a moon-filled night.

Kootney Plains

I am no Margaret Lawrence
though I wish her to be in my blood when I write,
leaning against the cold shuddering that takes me.
I was spineless, held together by Indian Affairs,
deposited at Drumheller, then Calgary, then
I took my heart to Kootney Plains.
I knew no other course.
In these rocky hills my mother and father
lived in a tent, tending horses and feeding on elk,
moose, rabbit, grouse and berries. For awhile
I found my family. I pretended all was right.
My mother was on crutches after one of my father's
solar flares. There in the winter wilderness
I rode wild horses, tore through the trees clutching
the horse's mane. It was then
the dreams truly began.

omāciw – hunter

I printed my name and drew a smile
beside the snowshoe trail
not far from the teepee of the blue-eyed stranger.
We'd spent a hungry afternoon
with hot rocks in the sleeping bag.
The following day my father sent me to collect him
to help haul our game.
He loaded a toboggan full of elk
and dragged it fifty feet until
it sunk through the snow's crust.
He lightened the load taking some of the meat off
spreading spruce boughs around it
he peed around the cache, left it for the night.
And we walked, five hours, five miles, sweating
struggling, my father pulling another toboggan and
I on snowshoes pushing behind the sled.
That night my father spoke to him in Cree
as if he was a son he had raised. It was the first
night my lover was allowed to stay.

nipiwin – from the dead

When I took his hand I thought I had left the garbage
pit only
I ended up recycling what I had learned.
I was a master at cutting the ground beneath my feet.
He was the first one to see the weight of my bundle
still
he'd draw me against his chest
until
the burn too scalded him.
I went to the healers:
of the medicine men, there were two.
One who took my worn-out feet and washed
them with his blood, the other
who gave me moccasins to welcome me to this trail.
The women came too.
They bundled the tempest in tobacco ties,
the one that shred my punishing soul
and nurtured me.
They pegged my lodge firm over the earthen hearth,
spread a blanket of sage.
The grizzly made a cape and danced
me back to health.

nīmihis – the dancer

After years of eating dirt
I still haven't acquired its taste
though I received vitamins from that earth.
I fell into the sink hole of my mistakes
yearning to dig myself out.
I stumbled to my first vision quest
where a spider spun its web in the entrance
to my lodge. From the dreamer's lips
I received my name.
Even though I am of the earth
tied to the spider's net
I dance between four heavens.
In spite of the Creator's comic web.
In spite of the guardians of the heavens.

pāstāhowin – crossing the line

In our way tiny pouches of herbs
are worn around the neck. I lost mine before I was born.
I have taken many winters to birth
this medicine walk.
Storms must curse and writhe
before the coming of light;
wihtikow has been blowing these four winds
for far too long.
She has left her tracks.
A Jungian was my guide. He opened the door
to the salted waters that filled his room.
His heart's the one that burst,
washed me of this pain.
In from this downpour of sleet and hail
my beloved clung
onto this rotten corpse
willing to wade
until I could breathe.

miyo-ohpikināwasowin – good child rearing

It took me a while to get used to his name.
It was as if I was taking my late brother,
the one who stepped out on the highway
into the winter night of a roaring truck.
My middle brother, my childhood rock.

Years ago I visited the graveyard on the reserve
and counted all the dead
from residential school; relatives, friends,
from my brother's life there were over thirty
of his peers: suicide, murder, trauma, fire
under the safe blanket of the rez.

Over so many years
and I still weep.

pimātisiwin – life

I have been freezing in this winter sleet
and wonder how others will look at me
after they read this rug I've braided.
I fear that community feast
will be nothing more than thrown stones.
I've placed feathers over this thin skin.
The arteries within these lines
echo the hidden walk.

kahkwēyihtamowin - jealousy

When he first took me to his home
it was clear I was from the wrong side
of the creek.
A blond arrived at his door, four nights
after my brother took his last breath,
and my newborn and I had flown home
to be at my brother's wake.

When he went to university
he spoke another upon his lips
a milk-skinned woman who had the language
he understood while
my tongue tripped on the accent
of my Cree.

For years I raged when I saw him
in the company of other women,
business suited women striding in high heels
while I stayed home, my high school transcripts
hidden and babies attached to my breasts.

nipēwin – the bed

My body writes across the sheets
in hopes that he will reach through these words.
I have been water-travelling in sleep
so many years
curled in his den
waking repeatedly to the sweet sweat
of our dreaming.

This is not my last water song
though drought moves through the small canals
within valleys of my womanhood
where I was betrayed.
Not by him
but by myself and those who believed
that power gave them access.
Not just me, but many small ones
sent to places where they were and are
still imprisoned.

I am exhausted, returning repeatedly
like a starving coyote
nibbling at my battered hide.
I wish to have ravens, crows, magpies
to deliver me good fire. A medicine tea
to soothe all my wounds.
What herbs are there for those
who still nestle in their duress?

I see it too often
thirty-year old mothers hurtled into hell
eight children lost to them
overwhelmed
fathers absent.
Men with empty wallets

arms filled with needle tracks
and dirty spirits on their breath.

The bed is empty this night
as I move my belly across its wilderness.
The landscape is cool and there is no scent
to distract me from my thoughts.
Many years. Leg over Leg. Head on shoulder.
Fingers clasping. So many whispers
that repair this suture, this wind-cut self.

mōyēyihtamowin – awareness

We lived in a teepee on the Tsu Tina Reserve.
My first born was two, sleeping in a hammock
between the poles above our bed.
I was chopping wood when I split
my finger, lips still burning
from my lover's mouth.

I was cleaning stove pipes with my son,
a small coal-faced bear,
soothed and tarred, when I felt my double's movement
so sly and slick
this ghost keeper that watched
from her dark sky.
She liked to shroud my vision.
I wrestled her before
she erupted, to spank this innocent
in the mess he made.

I drank in his child's light
and watched my shadow
turn slinking, dragging
in the ashes.

Two-faced

I started so many fires. I lost count.
I was an electrical storm waiting to breathe life
into the near dead embers
embedded in my belly.

My wardrobe was filled with many faces
yellow, red, orange and
halfway down that day
I'd change to blue, purple, and black.

"What do you think?" the medicine man would ask.
"It's up to you," another would say.
Think? Make a choice?
Slowly that horrific burn calmed,
thought and heart agreed
that one without the other
was a useless dance.

My children, others who have seen these loathsome winds
I wonder how many I have burned
in the cauterizing of my heart.

misasiniy - large rock

I have a rock with four nodules
attached like two sets of Siamese twins.
They are the four heavens of my universe
the family of four I was born into
the four that we are
the four seasons, the four directions.
It holds me when I am buckling.

No number of prayer beads
strung through my fingers
could release me from this nether world.
All I need
is to hold this rock.

Still I wonder
how long this possession will last.

nīpin nikamowin – summer song

I listened to outrageous laughter
there by the stone-carving shelter
where children painted and listened
to Alex Janvier.
Year after year
on the grounds of Blue Quills
I shared a tent with a friend and we told stories
of those lonely nights and how we preserved
our broken Cree.

I walked, ran, skipped
swore and sang the fourteen miles
from that school all the way to Saddle Lake.
We were told by our guide to meditate, be silent
in our walk. How could we after our voices
where lost in the classrooms of that school?
When I reached my home reserve
the Old Ones received me
and danced me on my blistered feet.
Water, tea, fruit, bannock and deer stew.
What food would heal this wound
bundled against my back?
A child still crying in those long school nights.
I know of a man who still carries his suitcase,
began at six, now sixty years, carrying
those little treasures of home
that was forever gone.

pawākan - dream spirit

Sitting in the darkness of my lodge
I found a round light
against my canvas wall.
It peered without sight
and I saw without knowing.
It was not the sun – *pīsim*
She paid no attention.
The moon – *tipiskāwi-pīsim*,
revealed its many ages
as its full face, her sight
travelled its long journey
toward my door.
But I could not be sure.

I was sitting in the forest
at the mountain lake
living off my lard
black ash on my forehead
listening to the walk.
Uphill I heard the anguished cry
of the one who hanged himself.
I was told not to pay attention
as this was not my walk.

The spider – *apihkēsīs*
the storyteller spun the cosmos
within my circle.
The earwig was my nemesis
her arrival was my discomfort.
Discomfort forced me to sit
in my shame.

I share this
because we are of the night

and of the flame.
The Old Ones caution
how we choose our path.

Hauntings

There is nothing that can keep *pāhkahkos*
these skeletal bones away
his thirty below fingers are constant caresses
all day, all night. His cat's tongue licks my neck,
his endless purr seduces me when I am lost
in memory.
I want to flatten him with my fist.
Squeeze his bloodless bones and wire his jaws.
I've offered corn, fish, heart-berries and fat
none of these appease him.
I've smudged with sage, cedar, sweetgrass,
smoked the Elders pipe and still he offends me.
If I can pull him over my shoulder, roughen him
up with tenderness then maybe we can make love.
But I don't like his grimaces, his disapproving stare,
his shrill voice reminds me of my thoughtless ways.
I've walked slow. Kept quiet. Laid still. Still
he thunders into my dreams, lifts my eyelids
pushes me down the steep stairs of myself.
I don't want to enter this dark hole
that knows.

I don't want to dance. Not here
Not with him.
Not yet.

pōni-āhkosi – quit the sickness

When you see the skeleton lurking in a tree
or standing on the road
leave him candies, strips of dried meat,
cookies, berries. Don't steal his kerchief,
like an old man he wears it around his neck.
don't lift a finger to steal his tobacco.
He honors the stillness, the waiting
he unpacks your memory
and makes you squirm,
makes you laugh,
makes you cry, brings you anger,
shame, regret
and at times he will share peace.
The Elders say, "It's up to you."

What do I want from him today?

Unpacking the Knapsack

I stood in the twilight no longer bound
by my brother's weight. I left his stains.
I've named the one who corralled me
in grade five, and returned his castration.
Left him to carry his own *pāhkahkos*.
For years I hoped the man whose fumes
suffocated me lay rotting in his dream
and wished my bald cousin who bound
my arms, my legs
was terrorized by his demons.
I think this of the one who claimed
he had the right to tear my limbs.
I wished his muscles would atrophy.
I hoped the man who drugged my beer
and left me naked and freezing
would think of his kids, as they drank
in the gravel pits.
I no longer have to witness
those greedy serpents. Yes,
all this and more to women's bodies,
to women's souls devoured
by *wīhtikow's* icy will.
Too many weighed down by *pāhkahkos*,
too young, lost on city streets.

Gossip flies tent to tent, house to house,
waggling tongues on rapid transit,
face-book, twitter.
The survivor is blamed. Me,
I won't wait for my skeleton to be found.
I've told
and my telling's been witnessed
in ceremony.

sakwahmo - hangs on

I have donned my war bonnet,
worn out my moccasins, my path
obscured by blowing dust. Sometimes snakes
sickened my path. Still
I moved toward some gray hope.
I've been like a compass needle
moving back and forth, to and fro
as the black winds raged in my hollow breast.
If I lived outside the healer's den
these crusted scabs would flake and fall.
I don't carry this loose meat gracefully.
I've earned it with a vengeance.
Lived life regardless of *pāhkahkos*, of
a bent over starving spirit, or
leeches burrowing on my flesh.

Like a sapling clinging to a mote of dirt
on the Rocky Mountains
I've clung through swirling winds.

I've smoked the sacred stone,
fed the heavenly souls. I take lessons
from their ancient trails, work to see
through their eye, sing their stories
from their throat, climb the mountain
of their lives.

If I wander on these pages, sift
these lessons through the lens
of my blindness
I pray those stories will move on
through my bones.

A Hummingbird

The air was cool. I stuck out my tongue
and suckled, and slept.
In the twilight trees quivered, a rock thundered
me awake. A hummingbird swooped,
hovered before the red prayer cloth.
A voice I couldn't hear drummed into my ear.
The rain pounded against the robe
I was wrapped in.
There were no other visitors those days.
Just dry, dry days
me thirsting, me wanting
to know. To know.

I want to know the vision of the rock,
hear the story of its long travel, gather
the lessons it wishes to impart.
I want to know the power of the hummingbird
how it handles it's long flight
what beauty, what turbulence it sees.
I want to know how I too can hover
to survey my distant journey.
I want to know how I can bring beauty
and drink the nectar of delight.

Four generations. My mother on the left, my grandmother holding my niece Dawn Half-Reid and my brother Peter Ivan Half.

Carry On

When the leaves were shedding
and the cool winds descended
we'd pack our pillow cases, heave
them on the yellow bus, leave home for school.
It was like sending us
to a foreign land, no familiar landscape,
no map to follow. We were stripped
of our clothes.
Stripped of parents,
brothers, sisters,
nōhkom, nimosōm
uncles, aunts
songs of the Cree, stories of our birth
the dances of the spirits.
Pipes and Lodges.

Some were strapped, whipped,
handcuffed and electrocuted,
bedwet sheets were gowns
paraded up and down the dormitory.
Others were forced to kneel for hours
in front of the urinals.

In the dark nuns made their lustful visits.
In the office a priest became the candy man.
Some were good students
and took these lessons home.

There are times when my walk
is the gall that I cannot swallow.
My hunting trails have been a crooked path
with turn-offs to hidden snares.

I'd find a struggling rabbit and
it became my food.
If I forgot the trail, I'd snare my foot.
Then I became the meal.

ēkosi – enough

I had enough as a teenager.
I had enough of the bar scene, the bartenders,
the blackouts, the vomiting, the hang-overs.
I had enough of the loose men, hotels, and
run-down shacks. I had enough of myself.
I wanted to ditch my blistered mouth,
my scorched throat, the dark desiring nipples,
my burning belly, the flickering between my legs.
I backpacked these.

This marrow is packed with the litter
of that wayward path.
I've traversed the interior
pulled by the hungry moon.

The Reserve Went Silent

The playground went silent.
A lone robin hopped in the expanse of the yard
where once children scraped their elbows and knees
drew lines in the dirt for hopscotch
or designated the imaginary rooms of a house
and lined the cupboards with mud pies.
The yard now empty, where once a lively
baseball field of excited runners
wore out trails between first base and third.
Where once the home base was a tattered
mound of scraped up dirt and scraggly grass.

I see this now.

I never saw the searing pain
on my mother's face, nor experienced
my father's eyes squeezed to dam his flood.
Their world went mute when the pied piper
played his organ through the reservation.
My parents never spoke
of the gash that tore through the families
and gutted the whole reserve

"When you fall, you don't wallow in self-pity. You get up."
Basil Johnson

My wind wanted to walk
into the depths of my oceanic dreams,
make them real as the flood of water
that would fill my nostrils and lungs.
I am frightened by water,
I can wade, fall in, float, paddle
and devise a breast-stoke.
But I don't have the stamina
to swim mile after mile. Waves scare me
though I have kayaked
the Bay of Fundy, with the whales beside me.

Water speaks to me. A low, ancient, guttural voice.
She scrapes my skin and I am always afraid
I will be sucked in. In dreams she tells me
to "ride the waves," or she will show me her
swimming snakes. Dark, murky waters,
sometimes clear, clean brooks.
I go back to her repeatedly
though my pocked scabby skin
is tattered with fear.
I've swum in her caves where people
where sacrificed, clung to my kayak
on the Saskatchewan River, her current
dragging my legs down
and my death chant silenced
in the icy roar of her breath.

I would not hang onto fear.
I could not or I would drown.

Lateral Practises

Some of us have learned the ways
of the supervisors, priest and nuns
from the thieving schools.
We took their bad medicine
as our own.
Evangelistic warriors within our midst
who command with stern tongues.
These Elders refer to us as the Nothing People.
True that many have nothing on their lips
except the jesus and his tortured life.
True that many of us are lost
with nothing but confusion walking
on our path.
We are like ants
gathering crumbs
dropped negligently by those knowledge keepers.
But
we haven't deserted all the way.
We offer our tobacco, hang our prayer cloth
take these small lessons
and reclaim them as our own.

The Quandry

I have stripped my soul of the visions, the dreams
I received, given them all away. Still I continue
to wait each day, every night for more to come.
They dance softly, reluctant to reveal for fear
I'd give again what I've received.
But if I don't do this what will you know?
Your bitterness will gnaw, when
what was needed went to the grave
without having been spoken.
nōhkom and *nimosōm* left us without their voice,
without this story of *pimātisiwin*, this culture
except the little that we saw.
Now I am a nothing person.
I cannot share what I don't know.
This endless search is meant to fill what I lost,
what is needed for this red road.
So I give these visions, share these dreams.
They have been my guides
in these many years of struggle.

Don't tell anyone of your visions, your dreams
they say, or they will leave you.
But my heart has no desire to remain tight-lipped
not because she needs validation
for receiving these messages,
not because she lacks humility.
She knows what it's like to crawl,
to beg to know
how to Sun Dance,
what offering she needed to make;
to know what to see in her Vision Quest,
what to expect. To know how to behave
at a Horse Dance, how to give at a Ghost Dance.
How to listen in a Shake Tent.

How to interpret the dreams,
these visions she received.
How can they teach, help.

Each day I am born again
to wander, to wonder, to listen,
to learn.

ospwākan - the pipe

He sat between the women.
Told the story of how the ancient Elders
taught white men and their native brides
that their half-blood children had no right
to the Pipe, to the ceremonies.
How this teaching applied to this present day.
When these people, he prophesied,
took their last breath
they would remain as wandering ghosts
disturbing the present peace of their lost land.

When the women
spoke of their ancient grandmothers,
spoke of being outcasts
and how this applied to this present age,
they spoke of their love of their mixed-blood children,
the love they shared with their men.
The condemnation that walked from that man's tongue
cut their blood line and spilled it.
They arose and left him
with his bitterness and hate.
Returned to their families.

nōhkum Adeliene Half – holding me and my brother Peter sitting on the floor with a happy face, My aunt Elizabeth Large holding my cousin Martin Half and the Desjarlais cousins.

April 30, 2014

Weeds are flattened beneath last year's tire tracks
others lay burden by the winter's heavy snow.
The crocuses labor through this thick blanket.
I am sun drained from the bleakness
of the weeks before. Now a tick
I've carried in my hair runs up my neck,
festers on my chin.
I show it no mercy.

The lake-ice is rotting diamonds
where water seeps hungrily through its cracks.
Beneath the birdfeeders
goldfinches and juncos scratch.
Two mallards strut
crane their necks for the roving dogs and cats.
Sharptailed grouse lay low in the thicket believing
they cannot be seen, their rust-colored wings
match the frost-bitten ground.

This morning we were woken by a knocking
on our skylight, the yellow feathers
of a flicker splayed against the window.
I cradle a striped gopher, it heaves so slightly
against my palm, a leg broken
and one eye bloodied shut.
I lay it against the mountain ash and beg
it not to suffer.

This afternoon I have my hearing
for Truth and Reconciliation.
I must confess my years of sleeping
in those sterile, cold rooms where the hiss

of water heaters were devils
in the dark.

I want to walk these thickets
to that far horizon and not look back.

Cave Diving

I don't want to go into the deep veins
of the earth where my fingers
will release the dark waters
or my feet step on the wrong rock
and cave the ground in.
It's hard enough that I sit
in her dark cave, fire glaring,
drenched in the hot steam of her breath.
I am not a miner marking
a calendar with sleep and hunger.
I am afraid that if I dive deep
the insane that wept in my dreams
will smear me with feces.
I already know that I am marked
and I reek with the collected spores
of moist dank musk.
How much can I take lying
open in this cave
while the vultures pick clean
what I hauled in?

kisēwātisiwin - compassion

My feet were in flames and I could not stand the sight
of my jailed, louse eaten spirit. For years
I sat with my therapists, having blown
in on my tornado. It was difficult lifting my head
to white authority, confessing yet again
trusting to thaw the layers of frozen mud.
And when I left my Goliath
lay like *wīhtikow's* decapitation. In the healing lodge
I wept while others witnessed my shame.

I thought my unwrapped soul
would never again enter these raging rivers
of melted memory. But the forest thrashed
me on this slivered dream
when my little people flared against me.
When I was in the monthly moon the werewolf
paced my prison. My forest had been charred
to stumps but still would be doused again and again
and again. And again and again I'd find my way
to another chair. But it was not confession to
those who listened, who wrapped my soul
in compassion.
They did not promise God.
They did not lie or twist in their hypocrisy
but simply
returned myself.

Burning in this Midnight Dream

I dream I wore a skin of X's across my chest
and down my torso. Granny prints of the midnight world.
Thick lenses moved inside my skull
magnifying but still I could not see.
The X awkwardly signed by my great-grandmother
another burned ink onto my skin for Treaty Six,
 X for the five dollar-a-year allotment,
 X stitched for medicine, eye glasses, teeth,
and for school.
X for every sin, X for moments of grace.
The X's of a long paper chain wrapped this body.

The tattoos beckoned me not to surrender
to wear a grizzly cape
to dance until the sun's flames and moon beams
created passion inside my womb.
I was earth, burning in this midnight dream.

Sentinels

Awoken from the sleeping forest I listened
to the distant arrival of sound. I listened
from far away to this arrival
of souls.
Their moccasins shuffling to the thunderbird dance.
They arrived from the dark sky, a trail
of brilliant night dancers, the swish of skirts,
a man's thump. Yes, here. In my bedroom.
Three months now, on many nights they would steal
my slumber. Finally I asked
what was it they wanted. Only
their muteness answered.

I travelled to the red baked soil
where the midnight people
with long decorated earlobes wore beaded chokers
and wrapped red plaid shawls around their slenderness.
I travelled east among the relatives who ate guts
and heads of animals, beetles, scorpions,
sea-urchins, sold dehydrated snakes, bladders
and herbs. They clogged not only their streets,
but the air I inhaled.
I burned incense at their temples, honored their gods,
spoke to my Creator.
Not done with roaming
I watched Mount Etna spew over
our car, rounded the curves of skin-tight streets
roved the full-breasted hills of Sicily
never certain where the roads would go.

Months later when all was still
in the thick forest of dreams I woke to the joyous
drum-beat of the dancers, they arrived
faster than I remembered, here quickly.

When the last leaf fell, my ancient mother
told my sisters and I,
"*ninēstosin*. I am so tired."
Her journey a landscape of sugar-beet fields
chicken-scratches and kitchen terrors
on her deerskin face.
The last small wind blew slow and gentle,
carried her as she planted a smoking rose
on all our mouths.

Solstice - the flame

Chickadees momentarily pick sunflowers
and flit twig to branch to birdfeeder
only to be crowded by flocks
of snowbirds dipping and soaring
unable to settle on a specific story.
Last night's solstice moon's full face
shone through our skylight.
The same fullness that lit
my spring fasting lodge. And on another time
after a women's night sweat,
lying in the dry grass
I saw
my grandmother, my auntie, my mother
my sister, my daughter and me
faces walking in her celestial light.

Owners of Themselves

"I have encountered so much silence.
Even when people came before the TRC
their over-arching silence
to me
overwhelmed the tidbits they were capable of offering.
I kept waiting
for their dams to break –
and hoping
that they wouldn't,
not right then,
not so alone
and far from home
I kept wishing
that every teller would have two grandchildren
beside them as they spoke,
a boy,   a girl,
so they could support the old people
as they fell into their dark holes
of memory,
and so they could also start to draw
the lines that connected the sense of self
of those grandchildren to the lives of those old people
started to reveal.
Until those lines began to emerge
and take hold, they could not call themselves
owners of themselves,
because they had to be given a history
to see themselves within.
They lived in simple,   unattached,   chaos,
far too many of them,
with so little control
over how they might respond
to anything."

Rupert Ross: is a retired assistant Crown Attorney for the District of Kenora, Ontario. He is the author of *Dancing with a Ghost – Exploring Indian Reality; Returning to the Teachings – Exploring Aboriginal Justice; Indigenous Healing – Exploring Traditional Paths.*

Left to Right: Auntie Elizabeth Large, nimosôm William Half, my father Adolphus Half and *nôhkum* Adeliene Half

Acknowledgements

In the course of writing *Burning In This Midnight Dream* I have not travelled alone. I am blessed with family and friends to draw strength from. It is therefore necessary to acknowledge the following people whose shoulders I leaned on. They provided emotional support and technical feedback. I owe them a lifetime of gratitude. They are Susan Gingell, whose respect for the work was so generous. Rupert Ross not only analyzed the text but heard through the deep pain of the voices and saw their movement toward healing. Ron Marken showed me again what poetry is about. Louise Million, a lifelong friend and therapist helped mend this soul. Tim Lilburn challenged the prosy noise I sometimes missed. I also want to thank Jean Okimāsis and Arok Wolvengrey for the Cree spelling.

I simply could not have completed these stories without my husband's ever present support and love. When the night demons robbed me of good sleep he was there. I couldn't ask for a more faithful, loyal, and thoughtful companion. I would not have written this story if it wasn't for the interest of my children Usne and Omeasoo. Their unconditional love, acceptance and my need to describe a history that remains present.

My brother Peter Ivan leaning against the door, my father Adolphus Half holding me as a child.

About the Author

John Lagimodiere

Louise Bernice Halfe was born on the Saddle Lake Reserve in Two Hill, Alberta in 1953. Her Cree name is Sky Dancer. Her first published poetry appeared in *Writing the Circle: Native Women of Western Canada.*

Louise has three book publications to her credit. *Bear Bones & Feathers* was published by Coteau Books in 1994. It received the Canadian People's Poet Award, and was a finalist for the Spirit of Saskatchewan Award in that year. *Blue Marrow* was originally published by McClelland & Stewart in 1998; its revised edition was released by Coteau Books in September 2004. It was a finalist for both the Governor General's Award for Poetry and the Pat Lowther Award, and for the 1998 Saskatchewan Book of the Year Award and the Saskatchewan Poetry Award. Her most recent work, *The Crooked Good*, was published by Coteau Books in 2007.

She was Saskatchewan's Poet Laureate for 2005–2006 and was awarded third prize in the League of Canadian Poets' national poetry contest. In 2015 Louise won second prize in the Written Awards category of the National Magazine Awards for four of her poems. Louise has a Bachelor of Social Work from the University of Regina and received an Honorary Degree of Letters (Ph. D) from Wilfred Laurier University in 2012. She currently works with Elders in an organization called Opikinawasowin ("raising our children").

She lives in a circular straw bale house outside of Saskatoon with her husband, dogs, cats and chickens. She is the proud mother of two very accomplished adults, and the grandmother to two very bright young boys.

Other titles by Louise Bernice Halfe

The Crooked Good
Bear Bones and Feathers
Blue Marrow

Printed in April 2018
by Gauvin Press,
Gatineau, Québec